A Catechism Of The Shaiva Religion, By Sabhapati Mudaliyar, Of Kanjipuram, And Sadashiva Mudaliyar, Of Chaturangapattanam: Translated From The Tamil

Sabhapati Mudaliyar

No. VI.

A CATECHISM

OF THE

SHAIVA RELIGION:

BY

SABHAPATI MUDALIYAR, OF KANJIPURAM,

AND

SADASHIVA MUDALIYAR, OF CHATURANGAPATTANAM.

TRANSLATED FROM THE TAMIL

BY

THE REV. THOMAS FOULKES,

ONE OF HER MAJESTY'S CHAPLAINS IN INDIA.

London:

WILLIAMS AND NORGATE, 14, HENRIETTA STREET, COVENT GARDEN.

Madras:

THE MADRAS DIOCESAN COMMITTEE OF THE SOCIETY
FOR PROMOTING CHRISTIAN KNOWLEDGE.

1863.

PRINTED BY GANTZ BROTHERS, ADELPHI PRESS,
175, MOUNT ROAD, MADRAS.

A CATECHISM
OF THE
SHAIVA RELIGION.

Part I.

QUESTION 1.

What is meant by the word Shaivam?

ANSWER.

All that relates to the religion of the God Shiva.

2.

Q.—What are the attributes of Shiva?

A.—He is eternal; without outward form; without passions; without external marks of existence; whose fulness fills all worlds; without any divine superior; unchangeable both in thought and word; without carnal desire; without enmity; and the life of all living beings. He is, moreover, immeasurably great, and spotlessly pure.

3.

Q.—What evidence can you produce to prove that there is but one supreme being?

A.—The world, which is his creation, is a proof of this.

For, if it be asked, whether this world is self-created, or the work of some being external to itself?

It may be sufficient to reply, that the world is an inanimate thing, and therefore could not create itself. We may therefore be certain that it must have had a creator.

Since also the creator of so great a work must necessarily be omnipotent, we conclude that he, and he alone, is the Supreme God.

4.

Q.—The Supreme Being is himself immaterial: how then was it possible for him to create this material world? and how, also, is it possible for us to form a visible representation of him so as to worship and praise him?

A.—In order that we might be able to represent him, and to serve and praise him, he assumed a concrete form, and concentrated all his divine grace in the supreme Shakti, who constitutes his left side.

In this form he is known by the name of Kailasapati,—'the lord of the sacred hill Kailasa.'

Moreover, in order to accomplish the three divine functions of creation, preservation, and final destruction, he exists in the three forms of Brahma, Vishnu, and Rudra.

5.

Q.—How may we learn the nature of the Supreme Being, the nature of the world, and the right way to worship God?

A.—From the Vedas, the Agamas, the Puranas, and the Shastras.

6.

Q.—Which are the Vedas.

A.—They are four in number ; 1. the Rig, 2. the Taittriya or Yajur, 3. the Sama, and 4. the Atharvana.

7.

Q.—Are there any other Vedas besides these ?

A.—Yes : the four supplementary Vedas, called,

1. The Ayur,
2. The Ardha,
3. The Dhanur,
4. The Gandharbba :

and also the six subordinate Vedas, called,

1. Mantra,
2. The Vyakarana,
3. The Nighandu,
4. The Chhandobisidha,
5. The Nirukti,
6. The Jyotisha.

8.

Q.—Which are the Agamas ?

A.—They are twentyeight in number. Their names are as follows :—

1. Kamika,
2. Yogaja,
3. Chintya,
4. Karana,
5. Achita,
6. Dipta,
7. Sukshma,
8. Sahasra,
9. Anjuman,
10. Subhrabhedaka,
11. Vijaya,
12. Nisvasa,
13. Svasabhuva,
14. Anala,
15. Vira,
16. Raurava,
17. Makuta,
18. Vimala,

19. Chandragnana,
20. Bimba,
21. Protgita,
22. Lalita,
23. Siddha,
24. Chandanasarvvottama,
25. Paramechara,
26. Kirana,
27. Bheda,
28. Vadula.

9.

Q.—Which are the Puranas ?

A.—The following eighteen :—

1. Shaiva,
2. Skanda,
3. Lainga,
4. Kaurma,
5. Vamana,
6. Varaha,
7. Bhavishyat,
8. Matsya,
9. Markandeya,
10. Brahmanda,
11. Naradeya,
12. Bhagavata,
13. Garuda,
14. Vaishnava,
15. Brahma,
16. Padma,
17. Brahmakaivartta,
18. Agneya.

10.

Q.—Are these Puranas classified ?

A.—Yes: they belong to the five following classes :—

1. Shiva-Puranas,
2. Vishnu-Puranas,
3. Brahma-Puranas,
4. Suryya-Puranas,
5. Agni-Puranas.

11.

Q.—Which are the Shiva-Puranas ?

A.—The following ten :—

1. The Shaiva,
2. The Skanda,

3. The Lainga,
4. The Kaurma,
5. The Vamana,
6. The Varaha,
7. The Bhavishyat,
8. The Matsya,
9. The Markandeya,
10. The Brahmanda.

12.

Q.—Which are the Vishnu-Puranas?
A.—The following four :—

1. The Naradeya,
2. The Bhagavata,
3. The Garuda,
4. The Vaishnava.

13.

Q.—Which are the Brahma-Puranas?
A.—The following two :—

1. The Brahma,
2. The Padma.

14.

Q.—Which is the Suryya-Purana?
A.—The Brahmakaivartta Purana.

15.

Q.—Which is the Agni-Purana?
A.—The Agneya Purana.

16.

Q.—Are there any Puranas besides these?
A.—Yes : the secondary Puranas.

17.

Q.—Which are they?
A.—They are eighteen in number; and their names are as follows :—

1. The Usanas,
2. The Kapila,

3. The Kali,
4. The Janatkumara,
5. The Sambava,
6. The Shivadharma,
7. The Chaurava,
8. The Durvasa,
9. The Nandi,
10. The Nrisinha,
11. The Naradeya,
12. The Parasara,
13. The Bharggava,
14. The Angiras,
15. The Maricha,
16. The Manava,
17. The Vasishtha-lainga,
18. The Varuna.

18.

Q.—Which are the Shastras ?

A.—The following six :—

1. The Vedanta,
2. The Vaisheshika,
3. The Patta,
4. The Prabakara,
5. The Purva-Mimansa,
6. The Uttara-Mimansa.

19.

Q.—Which of these relate to the Shaiva religion ?

A.—All of them: but more especially the Agamas.

20.

Q.—What special doctrines of the Shaiva religion are taught in the Agamas ?

A.—Amongst many others they teach of the three-fold class of existences, namely,

1. The Lord,
2. The Soul,
3. The World ;

of the four kinds of religious life, namely,

1. Religious services,
2. Religious ceremonies,
3. Religious contemplation,
4. Spiritual wisdom ;

and of the four degrees of future happiness, namely,

1. The presence of god,
2. Near-approach to god,
3. Unity of form with god,
4. Complete unity with god.

21.

Q.—What is meant by the expression 'The Lord?'

A.—The above-mentioned perfect, incomprehensible, and immaterial being is 'The Lord.'

22.

Q.—What is the nature of the soul?

A.—It is without size; eternal; sunk in the darkness of pollution; capable, in obedience to the divine will of the supreme god, of assuming a body in which it may accumulate merits and demerits; in which also whilst passing through the various experiences of this world, it commits sins and performs meritorious deeds, through which it becomes subject to a succession of births and deaths; and capable, also, by the help of a priest obtained at the time when its merits and demerits counterbalance each other, of being finally united to god.

23.

Q.—What is the nature of the world?

A.—It is uniform; eternal; of immeasurable power; able to conceal from sight all the soul's wisdom, as the rust on a drinking-vessel hides its brightness; subject to changes through the accumulation of Shaiva merits; and involved in darkness deeper than the darkness of night. For, the darkness of night makes itself visible, even while it hides the earth from sight: but this moral darkness both hides itself from view, and conceals also the Lord, the soul, and the world.

24.

Q.—What actions are called Charita, or 'religious services?'

A.—The following deeds are called by that name:—piously sweeping the temple; cleansing it with cow-dung; supplying it with lamps; planting a flower-garden beside it; weaving garlands and hanging them on the image of the god; attending the temple worship; frequenting the presence of the god; and reverently saluting the saints of Shiva.

25.

Q.—What degree of future happiness is to be obtained by performing these religious services?

A.—They who perform them shall dwell in the presence of God.

26.

Q.—What do you mean by 'dwelling in the presence of God.'?

A.—Dwelling in the heaven of Shiva.

27.

Q.—What actions are called 'Kriya,' or 'religious ceremonies.'?

A.—Performing the ablutions of great Shiva according to the ritual of the Vedas and Agamas ; worshipping him with offerings of sacred leaves and flowers; making oblations to him of incense and lights; and affectionately adoring him, and singing his praise.

They who perform these religious ceremonies shall obtain that degree of future happiness which is called 'Near approach to God'; which means, dwelling in close intercourse with great Shiva.

28.

Q.—To what visible forms may the worship of Shiva be offered ?

A.—To the mental image ; the earth ; paintings on wood, cloth, or walls ; sculptured images ; the stone linga ; the linga worn as a personal ornament ; the temporary linga ; and other similar forms.

29.

Q.—How is the worship of the mental image performed ?

A.—It consists in the mental performance of the anointing and other ceremonies of the temple-worship.

30.

Q.—What is meant by the worship of the earth ?

A.—The worship of the lord of the earth.

31.

Q.—What is meant by the worship of the temporary linga ?

A.—The worship of a linga made of earth for any single occasion.

32.

Q.—Which of these linga-worships is the most important ?

A.—The worship of the stone linga and the linga ornament.

33.

Q.—What are these linga ornaments ?

A.—Lingas which were originally worshipped by a devotee called Bhana.

34.

Q.—Where are these lingas found ?

A.—They are constantly to be met with in the bed of the river Kandaki.

35.

Q.—What benefits are obtained by worshipping them ?

A.—The merits obtained by bathing in the Ganges and the other sacred rivers : the merits acquired by pilgrimages to the different sacred shrines ; the merits accruing from the sixteen gifts of charity: and the merits resulting from the twenty-one kinds of sacrifice. Moreover it removes the guilt of all the greater sins.

36.

Q.—Which are the merit-bestowing rivers?

A.—These seven,

1. The Ganges,
2. The Jumna,
3. The Sarasvati,
4. The Nerbudda,
5. The Kaveri,
6. The Kumari,
7. The Godaveri;

to which are sometimes added,

The Indus, The Krishna,
The Tamraparuni, The Tungabaddri, &c.

37.

Q.—Which are the merit-bestowing temples?

A.—They are a thousand and eight in number; and are the same which those most eminent religious teachers, Tiru-Gnanasambandasvami, Apparsvami, and Sundaramurttisvami have celebrated in their religious poetry.

38.

Q.—Are hymns in existence at the present time referring to all of the above mentioned thousand and eight temples?

A.—There are hymns relating to two hundred and seventy four of them. Of these,

190 are in the Chora country,

14 in the Pandya country,
1 in the Malayala country,
2 in the Ira country,
7 in the Konkan country,
22 in the Nadu country,
32 in the Tonda country,
1 in the Tulava country, and
5 in the north of India.

The whole number, however, of existing sacred songs is eight hundred.

39.

Q.—Which are the sixteen gifts of charity?

A.—
1. Gifts of food,
2. Gifts of clothing,
3. Gifts of virgins,
4. Gifts of flowers,
5. Gifts of gold,
6. Gifts of cattle,
7. Wedding gifts,
8. Gifts of buffaloes,
9. Gifts of horses,
10. Gifts of white horses,
11. Gifts of sacred stones,
12. Funeral gifts,
13. The gift of the Mahameru,
14. The gift of the everlasting tree,
15. The gift of learning,
16. The great gift.

40.

Q.—Which are the twenty one sacrifices?

A.—Their names are,

1. Agnishtoma,
2. Atiyagnishtoma,
3. Yuktiya,
4. Jodasi,
5. Vasapeya,
6. Atirattra,
7. Aptoriyama,
8. Agniyadeya,
9. Agnishottra,
10. Tarisa,
11. Purnamasa,
12. Chaturmasya,
13. Nirudapasubanda,
14. Akkrayana,
15. Srauttramani,
16. Ashtakaiparvana,
17. Srarttam,
18. Sravani,
19. Akkrakayani,
20. Chaittri,
21. Asuvayusi.

41.

Q.—What sins are called 'the greater sins'?

A.—The following five;—

1. Murder,
2. Theft,
3. Lying,
4. Intoxication,
5. Contempt of the priest.

These sins subject the offender to the pains of hell. The following sins are also visited with the same punishment;—

1. Coveting a neighbour's wife,
2. Envying a neighbour's prosperity,
3. Desiring to deprive him of his property,
4. Anger,
5. Harsh words,

6. Obstinacy,
7. Deceit,
8. Forgetfulness of benefits received,
9. Dividing friends,
10. Unmercifulness.

42.

Q.—What is meant by the 'Yoga', or 'religious contemplation'?

A.—The withdrawal of the mind from its usual mode of communication with outward things through the five senses, and confining it to one single channel of communication: added to an ascetical course of life.

43.

Q.—How many kinds of Yoga are there?

A.—Eight: namely,

1. Yama,
2. Niyama,
3. Asana,
4. Pranayama,
5. Pratiyakara,
6. Tarana,
7. Dyana,
8. Samadhi.

44.

Q.—What degree of future happiness is attained by means of the Yoga?

A.—The degree called 'Unity of form.'

45.

Q.—In what does 'Unity of form' consist?

A.—In being like great Shiva, having clotted hair, a poison-blackened neck, four arms, and three eyes.

46.

Q.—What is meant by 'Gnana,' or 'spiritual wisdom'?

A.—The destruction of ignorance, and the knowledge of the truth respecting the Lord, the soul, and the world. It is to be attained through the kind aid of the teacher of religion.

47.

Q.—How is ignorance to be destroyed?

A.—By separation from external things, obtained through the initiation of the priest.

48.

Q.—How many of these external things are there?

A.—Thirty six: namely,

24 connected with the soul,
7 connected with knowledge,
5 connected with God.

49.

Q.—What are those that are connected with the soul?

A.—The 5 natural elements,
The 5 senses,
The 5 organs of sense,
The 5 organs of action,
The 4 intellectual faculties.

50.

Q.—What are those which are connected with knowledge ?

A.—The following seven ;—

Time,	Art,	Passion,
Destiny,	Science,	Individuality,
Illusion.		

51.

Q.—Which are those that are Connected with God ?

A.—The following five ;—

Pure knowledge,	The Shakti,
Dominion,	The Supreme being.
Equilibrium,	

52.

Q.—What degree of future happiness is attained through spiritual knowledge ?

A.—The highest state, called 'Complete identity'.

53.

Q.—What is meant by 'Complete identity' ?

A.—Perfect oneness with God.

54.

Q.—Which then is the most important of the four kinds of religious life ?

A.—Spiritual knowledge.

55.

Q.—Since spiritual knowledge is thus the most important of the four, what occasion is there for undertaking the other three kinds ?

A.—It is the divine decree that spiritual knowledge can only be attained after the performance of the other three.

56.

Q.—How do you prove that ?

A.—Those eminent men who have attained spiritual knowledge, have declared that they arrived at it after the observance of the other three.

57.

Q.—What have they said ?

A.—Amongst others, Tayumani-svami says,

" To those who seek the shrine, the fane, the pool,
The sacred priest reveals the deity.
The four-fold life of saints is as the bud,
The flower, the shell, the fruit : then God appears."

PART II.

QUESTION 1.

Q.—What miracles has great Shiva performed through his images in his temples?

ANSWER.

He has performed many miracles in all his temples at the sacred places. But it is only those wrought at some of them that have become universally famous.

2.

Q.—Which are they?

A.—At Tiru-Kadavur he appeared in the Shiva-linga on behalf of Markandeya, spurned Yama the god of death, and conferred on Markandeya the gift of always continuing in the form of a youth of eighteen years of age.

At Kalastri he appeared in the Shiva-linga on behalf of Kannappa-svami; and, when he had permitted him to behold him in a visible form, he took him up to heaven.

At Tiru-Vanaika he appeared in the Shiva-linga to a spider, and decreed that it should be born as a king. It was accordingly born in the royal line of the Chora country as king Kochengal-Chora; who, after he had performed many acts of religious service, became one of the sixty-three Shaiva saints.

At Kanjipura he appeared in the Shiva-linga to saint Sakkiya while he was in the act of throwing stones at him, and took him up to heaven.

At Tiru-Vidaimarutur he appeared in the Shiva-linga on behalf of the Pandyan king Varaguna, and bestowed his blessing upon him.

At Tiru-Virinjaipura he nodded his head to command a little Brahmin boy to perform the temple worship.

At Tiru-Valavai, which is the name of the temple of Madura, he appeared to many different persons, and gave them his blessing.

But it would be tedious to tell of all his glorious deeds performed for the salvation of his beloved disciples at different shrines throughout the country.

3.

Q.—Where are they all related in detail?

A.—In the Shiva-Puranas.

4.

Q.—Has great Shiva ever miraculously appeared in human form to save his worshippers from their sins?

A.—Yes, frequently. I will briefly relate some of these appearances.

5.

Q.—Which are they?

A.—At Madura he appeared in human form, and took the name of Ellamvallasiddhar. He changed old age into youth; he caused barren women to bring forth children: he healed the hunch-backed, the blind, the deaf, and the dumb; he enabled the lame to walk; he made a stone elephant eat sugar-cane: and performed many other miracles.

6.

Q.—Can you name some others?

A.—At Tiru-Vannamalai he became incarnate as the child of his beloved pious servant Vallalarayan, for the relief of the great grief which he had long been suffering on account of his childlessness.

At Tiru-Virinjaipura he appeared to some men of the Vaisya caste who were travelling that way: and, assuming the name of Marga-sahayar, he assisted them and protected them on their journey.

He also appeared in human form to Saint Tiru-Nilakanda, and changed his old age, and that of his wife, into renewed youth.

He appeared also to saint Chirutondar in the form of a Bhairava ascetic, and commanded him to make a curry of the flesh of his child. He then brought the child to life again, and took them up to heaven.

7.

Q.—Are any saints known to have been taken up to heaven for lovingly serving and praising this most merciful being, the one Supreme God?

A.—Yes; there are many such persons.

8.

Q.—Who are they?

A.—The sixty-three Shaiva saints, together with Manikyavachaka-svami and others.

9.

Q.—Who are the sixty-three Shaiva saints ?

A.—Their names are,

1. Tillaivarandanar,
2. TirunilakandarNayanar
3. Iyalpakai Nay.
4. Ilaiyankudimara N.
5. Meypporul N.
6. Viralminda N.
7. Amarniti N.
8. Eripatta N.
9. Enati N.
10. Kannappa N.
11. Kungiliyakkalaya N.
12. Manakkanjara N.
13. Arivattaya N.
14. Anaya N.
15. Murtti N.
16. Muruga N.
17. Rudrapashupati N.
18. Tirunalaippovar N.
19. TirukkuripputondaN.
20. Tandisa N.
21. Tirunavukkarasu-svami,
22. Kulachirai N.
23. Perumiralaikkurumba N.
24. Karakkalammaiyar,
25. Apputi N.
26. Nilanakka N.
27. Naminandi N.
28. Tiru-Gnanasambanda-svami,
29. EyarkonkalikkamaN.
30. Tirumula N.
31. Dandiyadigal N.
32. Murka N.
33. Somasimara N.
34. Sakkya N.
35. Chirappuli N.
36. Chiruttonda N.
37. Kararittarivar N.
38. Kananata N.
39. Kuttura N.
40. Pukar-chora N.
41. Narasingamunaiyaraiya N.
42. Atipatta N.
43. Kalikkamba N.
44. Kaliya N.
45. Sutti N.
46. Aiyadikalkadavarkon N.
47. Kanambulla N.
48. Kari N.

49. Nindachirnedumara N.
50. Vayila N.
51. Munaiyaduvar N.
52. Karalsinga N.
53. Idangari N.
54. Cheruttunai N.
55. Pukalttunai N.
56. Kodpuli N.
57. Pushal N.
58. Maniyarammai,
59. Kochenkal-chora N.
60. Nilakandayarppana N.
61. Sadaiya N.
62. Isaignaniyar N.
63. Sundaramurttisvami.

The following names also belong to this class :—

Poyyadimaiyillatar,
Tiruvarurppirandar,
Pattarayppanivarkal,
Mupporutumtirumeni-tinduvar,
Paramanaiyepaduvar,
Murunirupushiya-muni-var,
Chittattaishivanpalevait-tar,
Appalumadicharudar.

Several persons included in these latter collective names are individually of the above named sixty-three saints.

The chief of the thousand Brahmins of Chitambaram is also to be added to them.

10.

Q.—Have any of these saints performed miracles ?

A.—Yes : Tiru-Gnanasambanda-svami, Tiru-Navukkarasu-svami, and Sundaramurtti-svami, performed many miracles.

11.

Q.—What miracles did these three persons perform?

A.—Tiru-Gnanasambanda-svami, when going up to the sacred shrine of Tiru-Pachilachiramam, cured a young princess of her epilepsy by singing one of the Devaram hymns.

At Tiru-Marukal, another place of pilgrimage, he subdued the poison in the son of a man of the merchant caste, who had died of a snake-bite, and restored him to life by singing a Devaram hymn.

At Tiru-Kodimadachengundur, in the Konkan country, he went up to worship the god Arddhanarisvara; and when he had been there some days, the holy congregation was seized with ague, which annually attacked the people of that country at that season of the year. The saint sang a hymn in praise of the god, and so cured them of their fever. Moreover, he granted to the inhabitants of that country that they should never again be visited by that form of disease. The name by which that place of pilgrimage is generally known in the present day is Tiru-Chengodu.

At Madura he healed the Pandyan king of a fever by means of the sacred ashes, after singing the Tiru-niru hymn. And by singing another inspired hymn, he healed that king of his crook-back.

He sang another hymn on the banks of the river

which flows by Tiru-Kollamputur, and so caused a boat to float away of its own accord.

At Tiru-Vottur he turned a male palmyra tree into a female tree by singing an inspired hymn, and caused it to bear fruit.

At Tiru-Mayilai, by means of another inspired hymn, he transformed a bone into a woman.

12.

Q.—What miracles did Tiru-Navukkarasu-svami perform ?

A.—When the Buddhists cast him into a burning lime-kiln, he fixed his meditations upon the guardian-god of the place, and sang one of the Devaram hymns, and escaped unhurt.

They gave him poisoned milk to drink; and, through the mercy of great Shiva, he received no harm from it.

They let an infuriated elephant loose upon him to trample him to death : but the animal turned upon the Buddhists themselves, and slew them.

When they tied him to a pillar of stone and cast him into the sea, he sang the Devaram hymn of the five mystical letters; and, through the mercy of the god Sambavamurtti, the pillar floated on the waves like a raft of wood, and the saint was carried along upon it until he came to the mouth of the river Kedila, near Tiru-Padirippuliyur; and there he landed in safety. It is for this reason that the god of that place of pilgrimage has the name of Karaiyera-vittavar.

At Tingalur, by singing one of the Devaram hymns, he raised to life the eldest son of Saint Apputi, who had died of a snake-bite.

13.

Q.—What miracles did Sundaramurtti-svami perform ?

A.—At Tiru-Pukalur he turned bricks into gold by singing an inspired hymn.

He cast all the money which the god had given him at Viruttachalam into the river Manimutta, and took it up again out of the lily-tank of the temple of Tiru-Varur.

When he was on his way to Tiru-Vaiyaru in company with Cheraman Perumal, he saw the river Kaveri approaching, much swollen, and rolling downwards in a fierce torrent. He sang an inspired hymn, and thereby caused the torrent suddenly to stand still as if a dam had been thrown across its course.

At Pukkoliyuravinasi, a crocodile had eaten up a Brahmin boy some years before he visited that place of pilgrimage. The saint sang an inspired hymn and compelled the crocodile to come forth together with the boy, who had now grown in proportion to the years that he had been missing.

14.

Q.—What miracles did Manikyavachaka-svami perform ?

A.—While he was prime-minister to the Pandyan king, Arimarddhana, he was on a certain occasion on his way to purchase horses by the king's command. The lord of Kailasa appeared to him by the way in the form of a venerable priest sitting at the foot of a lime-tree, and gave him religious instruction. Then Chokkalinga-svami, the tutelary god of Madura, for his sake changed a number of jackals into horses; and he brought these to the Pandyan king.

Shortly afterwards he caused a great flood to swell the river Vaigai ; and then miraculously carried earth enough to dam up its overflowing banks.

He overcame the Buddhists in a controversy held at Chitambaram; and then bestowed the gift of speech upon the king's daughter, who had up to that time been dumb from her birth.

It is on account of the above miracles performed by them that these four saints, Tiru-Gnanasambanda-svami, Appar-svami, Sundaramurtti-svami, and Manikyavachaka-svami, are called, 'the teachers of the congregation,' and 'the lords of the way to heaven.'

The Devaram hymns and the Tiru-vachakam, composed by them, are called 'the Tamil Vedas of the road to heaven,' and 'the sacred code.'

The Tiru-vachakam was composed by Manikyavachaka-svami. The Devaram was written by the other three above-named saints together with some other holy men.

Natesa-murtti, 'the lord of the dance,' the guardian-god of Chitambaram, assumed the form of a Brahmin, and revealed the Tiru-vachakam a second time, which had originally been composed by Manikya-vachaka-svami : and, having written it out with his own holy hand, he commanded Tiru-Kovaiyar to make it known to the people.

PART III.

QUESTION 1.

Have any of the worshippers of the supreme Shakti, or Parvati, received special blessings ?

ANSWER.

Yes : an accomplished female musician at Madura affectionately sung the praises of the goddess Minakshi, accompanying her voice on a guitar ; and, for her reward, Minakshi promised her that she would be born as her daughter under the name of Tadatakai.

2.

Q.—In what manner did Minakshi become incarnate as her daughter ?

A.—This female musician in her next birth became the daughter of a king: she had the name of Kanjanamalai, and was married to the Pandyan king Malaiyadvaja. They were childless : and, when the king was on a certain occasion offering a sacrifice on that account, Minakshi arose out of the place of sacrifice in the form of a little girl of three years of age.

3.

Q.—What other persons have in a similar manner received special blessings for worshipping Parvati ?

A.—A Brahmin woman named Gauri was accustomed to worship Parvati, by constantly repeating the Gauri prayer, which her father had taught her, with great earnestness and love. Great Shiva, mounted on the sacred bull, and accompanied by Parvati, appeared to her in a visible shape, and took her with them to Kailasa.

A person named Kavirajapandita was also accustomed to sing the praise of the goddess with great devotion : and, as a reward for this, he received the gift of inspiration by which he was enabled to compose the hymns of the Saundaryyalakari hymn-book. Whosever shall use that hymn-book with faith and sincere affection, shall receive whatever good thing he may desire.

Another person, whose name was Abiramipattar, served the goddess with great sincerity. He was enabled to compose the Abiramiyandati; and, through the aid of Parvati, he caused the full-moon to rise on the night of the new-moon.

In like manner many other persons have received special favours on account of their devotion to Parvati.

4.

Q.—Have great Shiva and Parvati, who are thus so full of compassion towards those who worship them, any children ?

A.—Yes ; they have two sons, Vinayaka, and Subrahmanya. Virabhadra is also their son. Yet, though they are called sons, they are not to be regarded as distinct from Shiva, but only as different forms of himself.

Of Vinayaka.

5.

Q.—What was the occasion of the appearance of Vinayaka ?

A.—He became incarnate in order to destroy the infidel Kasamukha-asura.

6.

Q.—Why has Vinayaka the head of an elephant ?

A.—Kasamukha-asura had received the divine promise that he should not be slain by any god, demon, man, or beast : and therefore Vinayaka appeared in a body combining more than one of these forms.

7.

Q.—What is the history of Kasamukha-asura ?

A.—He was the son of a Muni named Magadha, by an infidel woman named Vibhutai, and was born with the head of an elephant. By his penances offered to supreme Shiva, he obtained a promise that all the gods should at all times obey his call, and that he should not be slain by any weapon, nor by any god, man, demon, or beast.

8.

Q.—What are the circumstances connected with Vinayaka's birth ?

A.—When the gods were sorely persecuted by this Kasamukha-asura, they made their complaint to the supreme lord. He was moved with compassion and determined to deliver them : and for that end, accompanied by Parvati, he went up to the painted hall which is in the midst of the forest on the slopes of Mount Kailasa.

9.

Q.—What took place there ?

A.—The portraits of Shiva and Shakti, which were among the paintings on the wall, were turned by the power of Paramesvara into male and female elephants ; and Vinayaka was born there with an elephant's head.

10.

Q.—How did he slay the Asura Kasamukha ?

A.—While Vinayaka continued to reside at Kailasa in this image-existence as the chief of the attendant gods and under the name of Ganapati, the gods persecuted by Kasamukha-asura, came in a body to worship him, and to complain to him of their great sufferings.

11.

Q.—What happened then ?

A.—Vinayaka took compassion upon them ; and, surrounded by the attendant gods of Kailasa, he went forth to war against Kasamukha. Remembering that the enemy had received the gift of immortality as above related, he broke off the tusk of the right side of his face and hurled it at him, and so laid him prostrate on the earth.

12.

Q.—What became of the enemy ?

A.—He did not die, because he had received the gift of immortality : but he changed the form of his body into that of a rat. When Vinayaka saw this, he leaped upon its back, and rode about upon it. It is for this reason that he is called Mushika-vahanan, or 'the rat-rider.' And, because he broke off one of his tusks, he is also called Ottakomban, or 'one-tusked.'

13.

Q.—What are his symbolical weapons ?

A.—An elephant-goad, and a cord. He holds the goad in his right hand, and the cord in his left.

14.

Q.—What has he got in his second right hand ?

A.—The broken piece of his tusk.

15.

Q.—What does he hold in his other left hand ?

A.—A cake.

16.

Q.—Why do the worshippers of Vinayaka take a lamb upon their heads when they go into his presence, and use the mode of salutation called Toppanam ?

A.—When Kasamukhasura was king, the gods were compelled to do him homage in those forms when they presented themselves before him: and so, when Vinayaka had conquered their enemy, the gods came into his presence with the same kind of homage, and petitioned him that they might thenceforth always approach him in that form.

17.

Q.—Were any other persons permitted to worship him in the same way ?

A.—Yes ; Ravana and Agastya.

18.

Q.—What was the occasion of Ravana's worship ?

A.—Ravana had been performing penances on Mount Kailasa, and had received from Paramesvara a Shiva-linga to protect the city of Lanka from destruction. When he was returning home with his gift the gods discovered the boon, and prayed to Vighnesvara to prevent it taking effect.

19.

Q.—What did that god do ?

A.—He called upon Varuna to overthrow Ravana ;

and, in the form of a Brahmin boy, he went himself to meet the monster.

20.

Q.—What took place when they met?

A.—Ravana, when he saw the Brahmin-boy approaching, saluted him, and begged him to hold the Shiva-linga in his hands while he went aside for a few minutes; and told him on no account to let it touch the ground.

21.

Q.—What did the Brahmin-boy say in reply?

A.—He said, "I am only a little boy, and have not strength enough to hold the Shiva-linga for more than a few minutes. If I get tired, I will call you three times, and if you do not then come to me, I shall be obliged to put the Shiva-linga on the ground."

22.

Q.—What followed?

A.—Ravana assented to this, and placed the Shiva-linga on the Brahmin-boy's hands, and went a short distance away from him.

23.

Q.—What did Vinayaka then do?

A.—The moment he saw Ravana sitting down, he called out to him three times: and, because he did not come at the instant, he put the Shiva-linga on the ground.

24.

Q.—What did Ravana do?

A. When he returned and saw the Shiva-linga on the ground he was deeply grieved, and snatched it up with his twenty arms. But a piece of the shape and size of a cow's ear was broken off and remained firmly fixed in the earth.

25.

Q.—What is that Shiva-linga called in the present day?

A.—It is called Mahabala-linga, because of its great strength. Its shrine is called Gokarna, because the Shiva-linga is of the shape of a cow's ear: for 'Go' in Sanscrit means 'cow,' and 'karna' means 'ear.'

26.

Q.—Did Ravana then proceed on his way?

A.—No; he became very angry, and struck the Brahmin boy, that is Vinayaka, on his head.

[Not numbered.]

Q.—What did Vinayaka do then?

A.—As soon as Ravana struck him, he assumed his own proper form: then he lifted Ravana up on his tusk, and tossed him in the air over and over again like a ball.

Q.—Did Ravana survive this?

27.

A.—He did not die, because he was a man of supernatural strength, and had also received Isvara's boon. But he was very much hurt and cried aloud, "O my lord, forgive the sin that I have committed in ignorance, and save me:" and then he worshipped him.

28.

Q.—What happened then?

A.—Vinayaka had compassion on him when he saw him thus worshipping him, and put him down on the ground, and said to him, "as a punishment for striking me on my head with your fist, you must hold up a lamb on your twenty hands." So when he had done this he worshipped Vinayaka, and having obtained permission to depart, he returned to Lanka.

29.

Q.—What was the occasion of Agastya worshipping Vinayaka?

A.—Devendra was once in great fear of the Sura, and left Svarga, and came to Sikari, and there planted a flower-garden with the intention of propitiating great Shiva. But there was no rain, and the flowers all withered away, and he was in great distress.

30.

Q.—What became of the flower-garden?

A.—While he was in the midst of his perplexity,

by the mercy of Shiva a miraculous voice from the sky said to him, "If a river were made to flow here, it would cause the flower-garden to flourish and produce plenty of flowers for the performance of your devotions."

31.

Q.—How did the river come to flow there?

A.—Devendra rejoiced greatly to hear this voice: and in the midst of his joy, the Muni Narada came to him and told him in what way a river might be brought to flow there.

32.

Q.—What were the means which he taught him?

A.—He said, "O Devendra, supreme king! the Muni Agastya has arrived at the mountain Jaiyagiri; and the river Kaviri is enclosed in his water-pot. If you will pray to Vinayaka, that river shall come and flow this way."

33.

Q.—What happened next?

A.—Devendra prayed to Vinayaka according to the directions of the Muni Narada.

34.

Q.—In what way did Vinayaka answer his prayer?

A.—Vinayaka assumed the form of a crow, and went and perched on the edge of Agastya's water-pot, and so overturned it; and the stream thus formed, flowed on to Devendra's flower-garden.

35.

Q.—What did Agastya do ?

A.—After he had overturned Agastya's water-pot in the form of a crow, Vinayaka assumed the form of a Brahmin-boy and approached the Muni. When Agastya saw him coming towards him, he attempted to box his ears.

36.

Q.—What happened next?

A.—He ran round and round, so that the Muni could not get at him, until he wearied him; and then he stood before him in his own proper form. When Agastya saw that it was Vinayaka, he was afraid, and fell down before him with the prostration of the eight members, and worshipped him. Then, by the god's command, he performed the buffeting-homage, and received the blessing which he desired, and departed to Mount Potikai.

37.

Q.—Has Vinayaka a Shakti in the same way as great Shiva has Parvati?

A.—Yes: he is united to the Shaktis, Siddhi and Buddhi; and he is therefore called Siddhi-Buddhi-Vinayaka. He is also united to the Shakti Vallabha; whence he has the name of Vallabha-Ganapati.

38.

Q.—Are there any special religious services peculiar to Vinayaka?

A.—Yes.

39.

Q.—When are they performed?

A.—On the fourth day after the new and the full moon.

40.

Q.—Are any special ceremonies performed on any of those days in the course of the year?

A.—Yes: there are special rites for the fourth day, after the new moon of the month of Avani; also for the fourth day of Angaraka; and for the fourth day, after a planetary conjunction.

41.

Q.—What holy persons have obtained future happiness through the worship of Vinayaka?

A.—The great Rishi Purushunda and other sages, Tiru-Naraiyur Nambi, Andar Nambi, Tiru-Venney-Nallur Mcykanda-Shivacharya, Auvaiyar, and many others.

42.

Q.—Why is it customary to worship Vinayaka, before commencing any undertaking?

A.—Because it is his province to protect such undertakings from all impediments. For this reason he has the name of Vighnesvara, 'the lord of impediments.'

43.

Q.—Is it proper to set him up for worship everywhere indifferently ?

A.—Yes. But the foot of the Vanni tree, [*Prosopis spicigera*] and of the Mandara tree, [*Hibiscus Rosa Sinica*] are specially sacred to his worship.

Shami, the daughter of a certain Rishi, and Mandaran, the son of another Rishi, were passing through a certain forest. There they saw the Rishi Purushunda, who had assumed the form of Vinayaka, and laughed at him. For this the sage cursed them both ; and they were metamorphosed into Vanni and Mandara trees.

44.

Q.—Was not the curse afterwards removed ?

A.—It was modified but not entirely removed. They have never ceased to have the form of trees : but they received a boon in virtue of which the shade of those trees has become specially sacred to the worship of Vinayaka, and their leaves and flowers are the proper offerings of his worshippers.

Shami and Vanni have the same meaning.

45.

Q.—Why is Vinayaka set up for worship in people's houses ?

A.—In one of his twelve incarnations, which took

place at Benares, he partook of a feast in the houses of all the inhabitants of that city at one and the same time : and from that day forward he has vouchsafed to be set up for worship in the private dwellings of his people.

Of Subrahmanya.

46.

Q.—What was the occasion of the incarnation of Subrahmanya?

A.—He became incarnate to rescue the gods by destroying Surapanma and the Asuras.

47.

Q.—What was the mode of his incarnation?

A.—Indra and the rest of the gods, when they were suffering from the persecutions of Surapanma, went to Kailasa and laid their complaints before the god. The lord of Kailasa took pity on them, and decreed that Subrahmanya should become incarnate to save them. Accordingly he assumed six faces, and caused six sparks of fire to dart out of his six central eyes. He then commanded the gods Agni and Vayu to take these sparks and cast them into a reed-pond. And those gods did as he commanded them.

48.

Q.—What then took place?

A.—Those six sparks of fire, through the grace of the lord of Kailasa, became six infants, and were nursed by the six mothers who form the constellation Karttika, [the Pleiades.] Then, when Parvati came to take them up in her arms, they assumed one united body having six heads and twelve arms. And thus he grew up; and the sacred names of Murukan, Karttikeya, and Gangeya were given to him.

49.

Q.—Why is he called by these names?

A.—He is called Murukan, because he has perpetual youth; Karttikeya, because he is the foster-son of the constellation Karttika; and Gangeya because he spent his boyhood on the river Ganges.

50.

Q.—What did Subrahmanya do when he arrived at manhood?

A.—He assembled his lac and nine brothers, who were mighty heroes, and with them diverted himself by performing many mighty deeds.

51.

Q.—How did these heroes come into existence?

A.—When the sparks of fire dropped out of the lord of Kailasa's central eyes, Parvati became afraid and ran away: and, while she was running, her anklets kept striking against each other, and the nine kinds of gems dropped out of them.

52.

Q.—What happened then?

A.—The image of Parvati was reflected in each of those nine gems; and those reflected images, through the omnipotent power of Shiva, became nine pregnant females.

53.

Q.—What followed?

A.—When Parvati saw this she became very angry, and uttered a curse upon them, that they should not give birth to their children. The nine females therefore shook with fear; and, out of the drops of perspiration which flowed profusely off their trembling bodies, a lac of heroes sprang into existence.

54.

Q.—Did they give birth to the children of which they were pregnant?

A.—Yes: sometime after this Parvati had compassion on them, and remitted the curse; and they gave birth to the nine heroes, Viravahu and his brethren.

55.

Q—What are their names?

A.—1. Viravahu,

2. Virakeshari,	6. Virarakshata,
3. Viramayendra,	7. Viramarttanda,
4. Viramahesvara,	8. Virarandaka.
5. Viramapurandara,	9. Viratira.

56.

Q.—What did Subrahmanya do?

A.—In accordance with the command of Shiva, he

took these mighty heroes, and with them two thousand companies of goblins, and came to this earth riding upon his chariot. Then he defeated and slew Kravu, Sagirya, and Taruka the younger brother of the Sura.

57.

Q.—What else did he do?

A.—He proceeded to Trichendur; and while he himself remained there, he sent Viravahu-deva as his ambassador to offer counsel to the Sura. But when he heard his arrogant reply, he departed from that place, and proceeded to Viramayendrapuri to lay siege to it. Then he caused Banuhobana, the son of the Sura, to be slain by Viravahu-deva; and he himself slew with his spear Singha-mukha, the Sura's younger brother, and also the Sura himself.

58.

Q.—What did he do after this?

A.—He abandoned Trichendur, taking with him Viravahu and his other companions, and the rest of his followers, and took up his abode in the temple at Tiru-Parangunda.

59.

Q.—What took place there?

A.—Devendra petitioned him to marry his daughter Devayanai: and he graciously consented, and celebrated the nuptial festivities at this place.

60.

Q.—Did he remain in that temple after this event ?

A.—No: He departed to Skanda-giri, and there lived in the enjoyment of the society of Devayanai.

61.

Q.—Did he ever leave this place ?

A.—Yes: He proceeded to the Valli-malai and there married Valli-nachi, who had been brought up in the house of a Kuravar. From thence he went to Tiru-tanikai, and dwelt there some time. Afterwards he returned to Skanda-giri, and abode there.

62.

Q.—What holidays are sacred to Subrahmanya ?

A.—The constellation Karttika, and the sixth day after the new and the full moon.

63.

Q.—What persons have obtained future happiness through worshipping him ?

A.—Narada, and other Munis ; and the emperor Muchukunda, and other kings.

64.

Q.—Who have been thus blessed in the present yuga ?

A.—Nakkira-deva, Arunagiri-nata, and some others.

65.

Q.—What sacred localities are there in which he

has visited the temples to confer blessings on his followers ?

A.—These six :—

1. Tiru-Parangunda, 4. Tiru-Veraka,
2. Tiru-Vavinangudi, 5. Cholai-malai,
3. Tiru-Chendur, 6. Kundutoradal,

and many others.

Of Virabhadra.

66.

Q.—What was the occasion of the incarnation of Virabhadra-svami ?

A.—Daksha in ancient times celebrated a great sacrifice without paying due respect to Paramesvara, the lord of Kailasa : and Paramesvara, therefore, determined to destroy that sacrifice, and caused Virabhadra to become incarnate out of his central eye, in order to effect its destruction.

67.

Q.—In what way did Virabhadra destroy it ?

A.—He took with him a host of armed ghosts, and slew all the gods assembled at the sacrifice, and cut off Daksha's head, and thus put an end to the sacrifice.

68.

Q.—Did not Daksha come to life again ?

A.—Yes : through the mercy of Paramesvara he did. But he was restored to life, wearing the head of a sheep.

The particulars of the history are related in the Puranas.

Of the established method of paying religious visits to Shiva.

69.

Q.—In what order is it customary to pay religious visits to Shiva?

A.—1st, the image of Vinayaka is to be visited; 2ndly, the principal linga of the temple; 3rdly, Sabhapati; 4thly, Somaskanda; 5thly, the Parivara-devas; 6thly, the principal goddess of the temple; 7thly, Chandesvara; and 8thly, Bhairava.

After the visit to Vinayaka, it is necessary to take leave of Nandi-deva before visiting the principal linga.

70.

Q.—Who is meant by Somaskanda?

A.—That form of Shiva in which he is accompanied by Uma and Skanda, is called by this name. This form of the god is also called Nayaka.

71.

Q.—Who are the Parivara-devas?

A.—Twenty-three of the twenty-five Muhurttas, consisting of Chandrasekara and his companions;—Sabhapati and Somaskanda being omitted: also Lingotpava, Dakshina, Brahma, Vishnu, Durga, Sashthara, Subrahmanya, Virabhadra, the nine planets, the eight Shaktis, consisting of Vama and her companions, and Paramesvara.

72.

Q.—From what point of the compass is the visit to be made ?

A.—If the sanctuary of the temple faces eastwards, the visit must be made from the south, that is from great Shiva's right-hand side.

73.

Q.—What if the sanctuary should face south-wards ?

A.—In that case great Shiva's right-hand side will be to the east, and the visit must be made from that side.

74.

Q.—What if the sanctuary should face the west ?

A.—The visit must then be made from great Shiva's left-hand side, namely, from the south.

75.

Q.—What if the sanctuary should face the north ?

A.—Then also the visit must be made from great Shiva's left-hand side, namely, from the west.

76.

Q.—What is the proper method of performing the worship of the Tvaja-stambha ?

A.—When the sanctuary of the temple faces the east, the prostration of the eight members of the body is to be made in the following manner :— the head of the worshipper must be placed close to the south-east corner of the altar of sacrifice : then his two hands must be stretched out northwards, so that the chest may touch the ground: in the next place both hands must be brought back and extended southwards, so that the shoulders may come in contact with the ground, then his two ears must be made to touch the ground.

When the hands are brought back southwards, the right hand must be moved first, and then the left hand: and when the ears are made to touch the ground, the right ear must first touch it, and afterwards the left ear.

77.

Q.—What is the rule for this worship in case the sanctuary should face the south?

A.—The head must then be placed close to the south-west corner of the altar, and the prostration is to be made in the same way as before.

78.

Q.—What if the sanctuary should face the west?

A.—The prostration in that case also must be made with the head placed near the south-west corner of the altar.

79.

Q.—What if the sanctuary should face the north?

A.—In that case the head is to be placed close to the north-west corner of the altar, with the feet extended westwards; and the prostration is to be made as before.

But if the visit to the temple is made after the fifteenth Hindu hour of the day, since it would be improper at that time to extend the feet to the west, the prostration, whether of the eight members or of the five members, must then be omitted, and the worshipper must perform his ceremonial visit in the standing posture with his two hands united and raised above his head.

80.

Q.—Why are visits paid at all to the temple after the fifteenth hour ?

A.—When an eclipse of the sun, or the sun's entrance into the zodiacal sign Capricorn, or any similar propitious occasion, happens after the fifteenth hour of the day, visits to the temple must be paid at the hour of their occurrence.

81.

Q.—Is the worship to be offered in the same form when visits are made after sunset ?

A.—It is only when the visit is made between the fifteenth hour and sun-set, that the prostration of the eight members is to be omitted : at all other hours, the worship must be offered with that prostration.

82.

Q.—Are there any other modes of worship besides the prostration of the eight members and of the five members ?

A.—Yes : there are in all five methods, namely, with

one member, with two members, with three members, with five members, and with eight members.

83.

Q.—What is meant by the 'salutation of the one member'?

A.—Obeisance made with the head alone.

84.

Q.—What is the 'salutation of the two members'?

A.—Obeisance made with right hand placed upon the head.

85.

Q.—What is the 'salutation of the three members'?

A.—Obeisance with both hands placed above the head.

86.

Q.—What is the 'salutation of the five members'?

A.—The prostration with the head, the two hands, and the two knees upon the ground.

87.

Q.—What is the 'salutation of the eight members'?

A.—The prostration with the head, the two hands, the two knees, the two ears, and the chest on the ground.

88.

Q.—What is the proper mode of performing the ceremonial circumambulation?

A.—Persons who are seeking to obtain a present

blessing, must make it on the right-hand side: but persons who are seeking for future happiness thereby, must make it on the left-hand side: and they who seek both present and future gifts, must make it on both sides. When a woman is with child, she must perform it very slowly, walking as if she were carrying a vessel of oil upon her head, and had her ankles confined in fetters. Fixing the mind intently on the feet of great Shiva, and holding a rosary in the right hand, the prayer of the five mystical letters must be repeatedly uttered; and when the worshipper approaches the presence of the god, he must lay his two hands flat upon his bosom.

89.

Q.—How many times in succession must the circumambulation be made?

A.—It may be made either three times, or five times, or seven times, or any other higher number which is a multiple of these numbers.

90.

Q.—At what times of the day must the temple be attended?

A.—At the three times of daily worship, namely, in the morning, at mid-day, and in the evening.

91.

Q.—May not the temple be visited at any other times?

A.—Yes: on the occurrence of an eclipse, at the

time of the entrance of the sun into the sign Capricorn, and on other similar sacred occasions, at whatever hour they may occur.

92.

Q.—Around which of the enclosures of the temple, is the circumambulation to be made?

A.—Around any one of them with the exception of the inner one.

93.

Q.—Why is the inner enclosure excepted?

A.—Because it is written in the Agamas, that no one may enter the inner enclosure except the Ati-shaiva Brahmins alone; and that they only may perform the circumambulation there.

94.

Q.—In what order are the different enclosures of the temple reckoned?

A.—The first enclosure is the wall of the sanctuary which contains the Shiva-linga: the second is the next wall to it on its outside: the third is beyond the second outwards: the fourth is beyond the third: the fifth is outside of the fourth: and the sixth is the boundary wall of the town.

95.

Q.—May not the Ati-Shaiva Brahmins perform the circumambulation around any enclosure besides the first?

A.—Yes, they may: and since the gifts obtained

by the circumambulation of the different enclosures, increase in the order of the distance of the enclosure from the sanctuary, the Ati-Shaiva Brahmins receive very special gifts when they circumambulate any of the outer enclosures.

Moreover, at those times when the shadow either of the steeple of the temple, or of the flag-staff, falls on any particular enclosure, the circumambulation must be made around some other wall outside of it. But on special religious occasions it is of no consequence, if these shadows should happen to fall upon the worshippers who walk in procession behind the god.

96.

Q.—Is there any rule about the length of time for the performance of circumambulation?

A.—Yes: the Agamas declare that a circumambulation ought to be performed for three hours; and that when it is performed for that space of time, the worshippers escape the calamity of succeeding births and deaths and obtain admission, at once into the heaven of Shiva.

97.

Q.—Is there any other mode of performing the circumambulation besides the one already described?

A.—Yes: when commencing the circumambulation, Nandi-deva is to be visited: then, leaving him on the left-hand, Chandesa is to be visited: then, returning by the same way back again, Nandi-deva is to be visited a second time: then, proceeding to the right until you arrive at the north limit, you return without passing the throne of the god, and visit Nandi-deva again: then proceed to your left to visit Chandesa: returning thence, you pass by Nandi-deva without worshipping him, and go on straight to the right until you arrive at the northern limit, that is the limit of Shakti: from thence you return by the same way, and, once more passing by Nandi-deva unnoticed, proceed to the right to worship Chandesa: returning thence, you first worship Nandi-deva, and then proceed to worship the Shiva-linga.

This mode of performing the circumambulation is called Soma-suttra Pratakshana. Worshippers who perform a single circumambulation of this kind, obtain an eternal reward. And when it is performed at the time called Pradhosha, it is attended with a special blessing.

98.

Q.—What is the time called Pradhosha?

A.—The three and three-quarter hours after the twenty-sixth Hindu hour of the day, together with the three hours and three quarters after sunset are called by that name. This interval is the special time appointed for worshippers to make their ceremonial visits to Shiva: and it is therefore indispensably necessary for those Shaivas who have received the initiation of servants of Shiva by means of the sacred ashes and the Rudraksha beads, to pay those visits at this particular time.

99.

Q.—What is the meaning of the word Pradhosha?

A.—It means 'the early evening.' In Sanscrit it is also called Rajani-mukhah. The Pradhoshas of the thirteenth day after the new and the full moon, are specially sacred: and on those days the special Pradhosha ceremonies are to be performed.

100.

Q.—Why is the thirteenth day of each lunar fortnight thus peculiarly sacred?

A.—When great Shiva in his form of Gangadhara, had vouchsafed to drink the deadly poison, he continued motionless like a dead man for the space of a kshana of time. It was then the eleventh day of the half-month. Meanwhile the gods worshipped great Shiva; and, on the next day, which was the twelfth of the fortnight, they broke their fast and satisfied their hunger. On the next day, the thirteenth of the fortnight, at the time of Pradhosha, great Shiva brandished his trident in triumph before Para-shakti, and danced his divine dance for the space of a Shama of time. It is on this account that the thirteenth day of the lunar fortnight is specially sacred.

Worshippers who visit Shiva on that Pradhosha must grasp the thigh of Nandi-deva, and repeat the mystical prayer 'Arahara' between the horns of the bull, which is the image of Nandi-deva, before proceeding into the presence of the Shiva-linga. The servants of Shiva who thus visit the god shall be rewarded with the degree of bliss called Shiva-sarupa, or, 'unity of Shiva's form.'

The Pradhosha of every Saturday is also declared by the Agamas to be peculiarly sacred.

Worshippers who visit the Shiva-linga must make their offerings of the flowers, leaves, &c., of the Vilva tree [*Cratæva religiosa*]. And whoever shall pay the price of the offering shall enjoy the same reward as if he himself had presented it in the temple.

They who perform the ceremonies of the Pradhosha must first pay their visit to Shiva, and afterwards partake of food: and it is very becoming for the initiated servants of Shiva to offer their prepared food to the god before eating it.

101.

Q.—Have any persons obtained future happiness by performing the ceremonies of the Pradhosha ?

A.—Yes: Chandra-sena, king of the city of Ujanimakala, through performing the rites of the Saturday Pradhosha, was enabled in the present life to subject all kings to his sceptre; and, after death, obtained the blessing of being gathered to the feet of Shiva.

Again, a man of the shepherd caste, when he had seen this king performing his worship, became himself devout, and erected a temple with all its appurtenances of the mud which he gathered off the streets: he then set up a stone in it which he regarded as a

Shiva-linga and worshipped it, and so obtained future happiness.

The history of these two persons is related in the Brahmottra-kanda.

Persons who undertake the Pradhosha rites, whether they are able to perform them thoroughly at once, or are compelled by bodily weakness to intermit them, must immediately make Uttiyapana. Should death occur before this is done, it appears that there can be no enjoyment of the reward of the rites. It is therefore very necessary to receive instructions how to proceed in these things from those who are well versed in the Agamas. This rule applies equally to all ceremonies.

102.

Q.—Is it proper to pass between Nandi-deva and the Shiva-linga when visits are paid to Shiva ?

A.—No: because to do so is one of the thirty-two offences.

103.

Q.—What are those offences ?

A.—1. Passing between Nandi-deva and the Shiva-linga :

2. Turning the back to the shrine in returning from visiting the god :

3. Going into the presence of the god with one of the hands closed :

4. Making only a single circumambulation :

5. Wearing the upper garment while paying the temple visit :

6. Walking over the shadow of the steeple :

7. Eating in the temple :

8. Sleeping in the temple :

9. Walking over the remains of an offering :

10. Touching those remains :

11. Touching the idols with the hand :

12. Touching the dancing-women :

13. Speaking to them, or looking at them :

14. Speaking vain words in the temple :

15. Speaking about things not pertaining to the temple :

16. Listening to others so speaking :

17. Speaking disrespectfully of worthy people :

18. Turning round to speak to unworthy persons :

19. Looking covetously at the consecrated property of the temple :

20. Worshipping the minor gods who are not mentioned in the sacred books :

21. Singing aloud the Vedic and other hymns and prayers :

22. Standing on a high spot of the temple :

23. Standing in the door-way of the temple :

24. Laughing at any person in the temple :

25. Praising hatred or any other evil disposition :

26. Turning round to listen to unbecoming songs :

27. Going to the temple at other times than the three seasons of daily worship :

28. Making the circumambulation carelessly :

29. Singing improper hymns to the god :

30. Spitting in the temple:

31. Blowing the nose in the temple:

32. Performing any other natural operation there. Similarly there are things which it is improper to do either in the temple pool or in the temple garden.

104.

Q.—What are they ?

A.—It is improper to spit, or to blow the nose, or to do any similar unclean thing in the temple tank, and also in the temple garden.

105.

Q.—What do you call the temple tank ?

A.—The pool which adjoins a Shaiva temple. It is to be regarded as the Ganges of Shiva ; and its water is to be bathed in as such, whether that water be clean or dirty. It is an inseparable portion of the temple premises.

106.

Q.—Why is the temple garden regarded with reverence ?

A.—Because it contains the flower-trees whose leaves and flowers and fruits are used in the offerings of Shiva: and also because great Shiva and the supreme Shakti have their dwellings in some of those flowers.

The details may be fully seen in the book of the Knowledge of Flowers.

107.

Q.—Is there more than one kind of Shiva-linga ?

A.—Yes : there are some which have been made by men, some by munis, some by gods, and some by the troops of Shiva ; and there are others which are naturally fixed in the earth. There are, therefore, five kinds of Shiva-lingas : and all five kinds may be worshipped.

108.

Q.—Is the reward of visiting them equal in respect to them all ?

A.—No : the merit resulting from a visit to a linga set up by the munis is greater than that which results from a visit to a linga set up by men : and so also with the others.

Though Shiva-lingas set up by men are mentioned together with the other four kinds, the men who set them up are by no means to be regarded as persons walking in the ordinary rank of men: they were Kshattriyas of the Chera, Chora, Pandya, and other royal dynasties.

These kings, on account of their special devotion to Shiva, together with their justice and other royal virtues, were favoured with the special and abounding grace of great Shiva. They also possessed the power of blessing and cursing.

109.

Q.—May Shiva-lingas then not be set up by ordinary men?

A.—When a village has no temple near at hand in which visits to Shiva may be paid, a new consecration may certainly be made. If, however, an old temple exists in a ruined state, it must by no means be pulled down, nor, in that case, is a new consecration necessary. But no private individual is permitted to set himself up as proprietor of such a temple; for the Agamas declare that in such cases Ati-Shaiva Brahmins alone shall be elected proprietors.

110.

Q.—When a new temple is about to be built, may its founders bring an unfrequented linga from some neighbouring place and set it up in such new temple?

A.—If the linga is an artificially made one it may not be so removed. But if it is a natural one it may.

On this subject, however, the Agamas must be carefully consulted.

111.

Q.—But is not the natural linga firmly fixed in the earth? How then can it be removed?

A.—The natural lingas just referred to are such as resemble artificially made ones, though they are in truth naturally formed. They are called Kasi-lingas, and Bhana-lingas.

112.

Q.—What is to be done in case of misfortune happening to any of those temples upon which hymns have been composed?

A.—At such times if the original object of worship should be in danger of being destroyed, another temple may be chosen, and the Shiva-linga must be removed into it; but if it cannot be destroyed, though another linga be elsewhere set up to represent it, the original linga must still be regarded as the proper object of worship.

113.

Q.—In what kind of Shiva-linga does great Shiva specially dwell?

A.—He is invariably present in the natural linga.

114.

Q.—Since great Shiva is omnipresent and fills all space, what illustration can you give to shew that he dwells in the Shiva-linga of the temples?

A.—Milk pervades the whole body of the cow; and yet it is in her udder alone that it concentrates itself visibly. So great Shiva specially dwells in the Shiva-linga.

115.

Q.—How is it that great Shiva has taken to himself temples to dwell in the so many distinct sacred places?

A.—Inasmuch as there are so many distant and

distinct countries throughout the land, the people would have had much difficulty in enjoying their visits to Shiva, if he had not thus taken to himself many temples for his abode. Moreover, it is stated in the Kanji-purana, that Parvati once asked great Shiva, why he had so many dwelling-places in the earth ? And that great Shiva graciously replied, that he dwelt in so many temples in order that his worshippers scattered throughout all countries, might everywhere be able to come into his presence.

116.

Q.—Is it mentioned what special reward attends the visit to Shiva at each of the three appointed times of daily worship ?

A.—If the visit is made at the time of the morning worship, the sins committed on that particular day, shall be blotted out : visits made at the time of the mid-day worship, blot out the sins of the worshipper's present birth : and if the visits are made at the time of the evening worship, the sins of succeeding births shall be blotted out.

117.

Q.—Why is the Ganges considered more sacred than all other rivers ?

A.—Because that river is the position of the fingers of the goddess Parvati.

118.

Q.—How did it become the place of her fingers ?

A.—On a certain occasion when Parvati was walking behind her lord, and great Shiva's two eyes were closed, the river sprang from her ten fingers.

119.

Q.—For what reason did great Shiva adorn his sacred hair with the Ganges?

A.—The Ganges having so originated, became a mighty rushing torrent, as if the seven seas had mingled their troubled waves together; and through a thousand different outlets, it poured itself forth to overflow the whole earth. Brahma, and the rest of the gods, when they saw it, were overwhelmed with fear, and hastened to Kailasa to lay their complaints before the god. He had compassion upon them; and by his sacred will, he compelled the great torrent to roll itself back again; and then he wrapped up the contracted waters in the crown-tuft of his hair, just as if it had been a single drop of rain.

For this reason, Shiva has the name of Gangadhara.

He is also called Chandra-sekara, because he wears the moon as an ornament in his tuft of hair.

120.

Q.—How came the Ganges to descend to this earth?

A.—It was brought down by a king, whose name was Bhagiratha.

121.

Q.—Why does Shiva wear the moon in his hair?

A.—When Daksha had given his twenty-seven

daughters to Chandra, he dismissed him with the command to treat them all with equal affection. Notwithstanding, Chandra specially favoured two of his wives, Karttika and Rohani, who were more beautiful than the rest, and neglected the other twenty-five. They were much grieved, and went to tell their father Daksha of it. The sage became very angry, and uttered a curse upon Chandra, condemning him to lose the sixteen parts into which he is divided one after another. Chandra saw one of his parts failing him day after day to the extent of fifteen of them; and then in great sadness he appealed to Devendra. But that god replied, that he was unable to remove the curse. He then went to tell his grief to Brahma. That god replied, "Though I should command Daksha to remove the curse, he will not obey me: but if you will go to the holy hill of Kailasa and there make your prayer to mighty Shiva, this curse may be removed." When Chandra heard this, he hastened to Kailasa and worshipped great Shiva and sang his praise. Great Shiva had mercy upon him, and took the sixteenth part of Chandra which remained of him, and bound it up in his crown-tuft of hair, saying, "If this were to remain in thy possession, Daksha's curse would destroy it with the rest that have gone: but henceforth that curse cannot pursue this portion, so long as it remains wrapped up in my hair. And because this portion is undestroyed, thy other lost portions shall be added to it again one by one in the same manner that they were destroyed. Nevertheless, though thou shalt thus gradually recover them all once more, they shall continue successively to decrease and to increase henceforward for ever." Chandra rejoiced to hear these words: and when he had sung the praises of the god, and obtained his leave to depart, he returned to his own abode.

122.

Q.—Why does great Shiva carry a deer in one of his sacred hands?

A.—That deer was driven towards him in the Taruka forest by the Rishis.

On a certain occasion in ancient times, great Shiva condescended to visit the Taruka forest in the form of a religious mendicant. When the wives of the Rishis saw his beauty, they fell in love with him, and were in danger of losing their virtue. The Rishis perceiving this, became very angry with the stranger and sought to destroy him. They first dug a sacrificial pit, and by their magical arts they caused a tiger to rush out of it to tear their enemy to pieces. But he slew it, and took its skin and wrapped it about him for a garment. Then they caused a deer to spring out of the pit: but he graciously took it up in his left hand, and has ever since retained it there. Then they produced a rod of red-hot iron, and caused it to approach him: this also he took up, and kept in his hand as one of his weapons. They next caused serpents to appear, and drove them upon him: but these he strung about his person for ornaments. Then they brought the Asura Muyalkatocombat with him : butas soon ashe approached him, he hurled him to the ground, and mounted upon his back, and stood there. Then they produced their incantations and hurled them at him : but these he turned into their own proper bodily form, and retained them in his sacred hand.

123.

Q.—Why does he wear the chaplet containing a boar's tusk, a tortoise, and the bone of a fish's eye, and carry a skull in his hand ?

A.—Vishnu, having assumed his fish incarnation in the sea, slew the Asura who had stolen and carried away the Vedas. He then swallowed the torrent of blood, and became like a drunken man : and the world was afflicted on account of the polluted state of the ocean. Upon this, the gods went to Kailasa and made known the matter which had brought them thither by their prayers for relief. The god had compassion upon them, and sent a Bhairava to deliver them, who went and cast a net into the sea and caught the eyes of the fish and brought them to his lord ; and Shiva placed them in his bosom at the request of the gods.

2. He wears the tortoise for the following reason :—When the gods began to churn the ocean of milk to produce ambrosia, using the hill Mantra for a churning-staff, and the serpent Vasuki for a rope, the hill sank into the ocean. The gods therefore sang the praise of Vishnu, and he came to their relief in the form of a tortoise, and caused the hill to rest upon his back. But in so doing, he disturbed the waters and mixed up the materials of the ambrosia. When the gods saw this, they hastened to the lord of Kailasa, and made known their petitions to him. The god had pity upon them, and sent Vinayaka to help them. Vinayaka came and put out his trunk and drank up all the water of the sea : and in doing so, the tortoise also entered his trunk. Vinayaka then cast up the water again ; and the tortoise came forth with it and fell to the earth in a great rage. When Vinayaka saw it he caught it by its shell on his tusk, and brought it as an offering to Shiva. The god was glad, and at the request of the gods he placed it in his bosom with his chaplet of skulls.

3. He wears a boar's tusk for the following reason :—A certain Asura named Hiranyaksha had obtained the favour of Brahma on account of his penances: in consequence of which he went about ravaging the earth. When Vishnu heard of this, he assumed the incarnation of the boar, and slew

him, and became intoxicated with pride on account of his victory. The gods, therefore, went to the lord of Kailasa to make their petitions to him: and great Shiva vouchsafed his favour towards them, and sent Subrahmanya to their relief. Subrahmayna smote the boar on the head with his spear, and pinned it to the ground: then he plucked out its tusk, and carried it into the presence of Shiva, and he has ever since worn it on his person as an ornament.

124.

Q.—Why does he wear a necklace of bones and a chaplet of skulls?

A.—Having caused Brahma and Vishnu to come into existence, he created the world through the instrumentality of Brahma, and preserves it through the instrumentality of Vishnu; and at the end of each appointed time, he destroys it. In the exercise of these three divine functions, in due course he destroyed Brahma and Vishnu with the rest of the Creation, but it pleased him to wear their bones and their skulls as garlands. And he did this out of kindness towards them, and not from pride.

At the end of one of the early kalpas, he reduced them to ashes by a spark emitted out of his central eye: and he rubbed their ashes upon his sacred body for beauty. This also was an act of bounteous mercy intended for their good.

In former times Brahma fell into a state of proud presumptuousness: and, in order to restrain this, Shiva plucked off the central head of that god's five heads, and has ever since been pleased to carry the skull in his hand. From that time, Brahma is known by the name of 'The four-headed.'

On account of wearing a chaplet of skulls, great Shiva is called 'Shira-mali': and he has the name of 'Kapali' because he carries a skull in his hand.

125.

Q.—Why has he the black mark of poison stained on his neck?

A.—While the gods were churning the sea of milk for the ambrosia, a deadly poison was produced in it. When they saw it, they prayed to Shiva; and in order to save them from its effects, he drank the poison and deposited it in his neck. On this account he has the names, 'Kalakanda,' 'Karaimidattan' and 'Nilakanda.'

126.

Q.—Why does great Shiva ride on a bull?

A.—In former times Dharma-deva, seeing the downfall of Brahma, Vishnu, and the rest of the gods, and being desirous of an endless existence for himself, took the form of a bull and came to great Shiva and worshipped him, saying, "My lord, graciously accept your humble slave for your vehicle, in order that I may ever be preserved from death;" and he sang the praise of the god. Then Shiva of his goodness, condescended to accept him for his vehicle.

Moreover, Vishnu, on a certain occasion, took the form of a bull, and obtained as a boon from the lord of Kailasa to be accepted as his vehicle in that form.

127.

Q.—Why does great Shiva wear an Elephant's hide for his cloak?

A.—A certain Asura named Gaya, who appeared in the form of an elephant, performed great penances in honour of Brahma, and asked as his reward that he might be enabled to conquer the gods and to triumph over them all. Brahma granted him that boon, and with it gave him a command to avoid meeting great Shiva face to face, lest the boon should lose its power. He then made war upon Devendra and his followers, and conquered them. On his return the Munis saw him and fled away in alarm to Benares. He also followed them thither. When they saw him they were in great terror and entered the temple called Manikarnikai, and took great Shiva for their refuge. Gaya now forgot the warning of Brahma, and because his time was approaching its end, he followed them into the temple. While he was in the act of roaring aloud that he would slay the Munis, the god in his wrath assumed the form of Ugra, and trampled on the head of Gaya, and ripped up his body, and stripped off his hide, and cast it over his shoulders for a cloak.

128.

Q.—Nandi-deva is called the guardian of Kailasa: what is his history ?

A.—He became incarnate as the son of the Muni Siladhara as the reward of the penances of that sage. In due time, he lived as an ascetic on the banks of the sacred river Vaiyar ; and there, through the grace of great Shiva, he became possessed of the deer, the rod of hot iron, the blackened throat, and the other characteristics of Shiva. He also conferred upon him the silver stick and the short sword ; and with them Nandi was installed in the office of guardian, and so became the chief of the hosts of Shiva.

129.

Q.—Why are the sacred ashes and Rudraksha beads [berries of the *Elæocarpus*] considered of importance in the Shaiva religion. ?

A.—Because they are worn by great Shiva upon his sacred body, and in his sacred eyes.

[Not numbered.]

Q.—What is the origin of the sacred ashes ?

A.—The sacred body of Shiva is covered with the ashes naturally ; in this form it is called 'the eternal ashes.' In the next place, after he has reduced the gods together with all animate and inanimate things to ashes at the end of each kalpa, he rubs their ashes upon his sacred body ; in this form it is called 'the original ashes.' And since the god thus adorns his sacred body, they only can be the true servants of Shiva who constantly wear the sacred ashes rubbed upon their person.

The reward of so doing is declared in the Agamas to be the blotting out of all the greater sins. They also teach that the ashes to have this effect must be made of cow-dung : and that there are three methods of preparing it, namely, Kalpa, Anakalpa, and Upakalpa : and that no other ashes but such as is made in one of these three ways must be rubbed on the body.

130.

Q.—What is the Kalpa method ?

A.—The best of the cows which have been fed upon rice-straw in the month of Panguni are to be brought into a purified cow-shed; and their dung must be collected upon lotus-leaves before it touches the ground. Then the upper portion of it must be laid aside and made into a ball. This ball is to be put into the fire of Shiva, which is to be kindled beforehand. When it has been burnt for a sufficient time, it must be removed and laid up in a new pot: and any quantity of the ashes that may be required for use must be placed in the temple. Then, if it be smeared upon the body without any particle of it being permitted to fall to the ground, the affliction of successive births and deaths shall cease, and heavenly bliss shall be obtained.

The ashes thus made is called 'Kalpa-vidhi.' While the cow-dung is being collected, while it is being cast into the fire, while it is being removed after having been burnt, and also while it is being placed in the new pot, an appointed form of prayer is to be used. This form of prayer must be learnt from the priest.

131.

Q.—What is the Anakalpa method ?

A.—By this method the ashes is made of dry cow-dung gathered in the fields, pounded, mingled with the urine of the cow, kneaded, and thrown into the fire of Shiva.

132.

Q.—What is the Upa-kalpa method ?

A.—By this method any common ashes is mingled with the ashes of the kitchen of a Shaiva temple, moistened with the urine of the cow, kneaded, made into a ball, and cast into the fire of Shiva whenever it may be required, and after being placed in a Shaiva temple, it may be rubbed on the body.

133.

Q.—In what covering must the ashes be laid up in the temple ?

A.—In a garment, or in the skin of a tiger or a deer. Or it may be placed in a small bag ; but in nothing else.

134.

Q.—Why is the cow more sacred than all other animals?

A.—Because she yields all things necessary to enable the Munis and the gods to dwell by the side of the sacred rivers and pools : and also because she belongs to the same species as the cow of paradise, which produces all that the gods desire.

135.

Q.—Upon what parts of the body must the sacred ashes be rubbed ?

A.—Upon the crown of the head, the forehead, the chest, the stomach, the knees, and the back, in three horizontal stripes.

Directions for doing this, together with the appointed forms of prayer to be used while applying the ashes, are taught by the priest at the time of initiation.

136.

Q—Why must the ashes be put on in three horizontal stripes ?

A.— As a visible sign that by the ashes the three kinds of spiritual pollution are removed, namely, pride, sinful actions, and deceit.

137.

Q.—Is there more than one kind of initiation?

A.—Yes: there are three kinds : 1. The Samaya-diksha, or ordinary sectarial initiation; 2. The

Visheshya-diksha, or special initiation; and 3. The Nirvana-diksha, or heavenly initiation.

The Samaya-diksha is bestowed upon all the members of the sect indiscriminately: the other two are only bestowed upon disciples after their qualifications have been well ascertained.

The first of the three is called Samayadiksha, because by it a person is made a member of the Shaiva sect. The second is called Visheshya-diksha, because it surpasses the Samayadiksha in degree. The third is called Nirvana-diksha, because it bestows heavenly bliss : for Nirvana is one of the names of future happiness.

138.

Q.—Of what caste must the priests be who confer these initiations ?

A.—They must be Brahmins of the Ati-Shaiva sect by birth, invested with the sacred cord, initiated with all three forms of initiation, and ordained priests.

When such a priest has learnt by heart a hundred thousand verses of the Agamas, he is entitled to be called 'a priest of the highest order' :— when he can repeat fifty thousand, he is placed in the middle order: but so long as he knows only twenty thousand verses, he is classed in the lower order of priests.

139.

Q.—To wear the sacred ashes seems to be of itself

sufficient : why then are the Rudraksha beads worn also?

A.—The sacred ashes and the Rudraksha beads together are the characteristic symbols of Shiva; and, for that reason, they must both be worn. Besides, the ashes may occasionally be effaced by perspiration or rain; but the Rudraksha beads will still remain to save the man from transgressing and to keep away the sin with which the Rakshasas torment mankind.

140.

Q.—Where, and in what way, did the Rudrakshas originate ?

A.—When great Shiva was on his way to destroy the three cities called Tripura, in his overflowing passion tears rolled from his eyes ; and those tears became Rudraksha beads. It is on that account that they are called Rudrakshas ; for ' Rudra' is one of the names of Shiva, and ' Aksha,' means ' eye,' and also ' the eye-ball.'

They who conduct the temple-worship of Shiva, must of necessity wear the Rudraksha beads ; otherwise great Shiva will not accept their worship.

141.

Q.—How many Rudrakshas are to be worn?

A.—One bead on the crown of the head; six beads on each ear; forty around the head; thirty-two on the neck; a hundred and eight on the chest, thirty-two on the arms; and twenty-four in the hands.

142.

Q.—May any other beads be strung together with the Rudrakshas?

A.—Yes: coral, diamonds, and beads of gold must be strung between them: and the broken nuts of the Vilva tree may also be added to these. But if the Rudrakshas be strung alone, the reward will be merely that of wearing a single bead whatever the number upon the string may be. Whether the Rudrakshas which a priest wears in performing the temple service have a single face, five faces, eleven faces, or fourteen faces, the reward will be the same, namely, that of performing the worship of Shiva.

143.

Q.—How is it possible for animals and other irrational creatures to acquire Shaiva merits by wearing the ashes and Rudrakshas, and by paying religious visits to Shiva and worshipping him?

A.—Paramesvara, in the age of the first creation of souls in their primæval solitude, when they existed without material bodies and apart from all material circumstances, took to himself a body to be their temple, their sin-cleansing pool, and a visible object of worship. He then ordained, that even worms and similar inferior creatures which might be born, dwell, or die in Shaiva temples, should possess Shaiva merits; that fish and other aquatic creatures born, living, or dying in the waters of the sacred rivers and pools, and four-footed beasts and men, and all kind of birds drinking or bathing in them, or having even their drops of spray sprinkled upon them, should possess similar merits; and that rice-corn and other grains irrigated by those sacred waters and nourished by them, and birds feeding on the grain so grown, should also partake of those merits. He then created all kinds of trees, rice and every other kind of grain, cattle and all other beasts, fit to be used in the religious unctions of the mighty Linga, in the temple worship, as the offerings of worshippers, and for all other sacred purposes: and, lastly, he created the merits attached to these things.

144.

Q.—In what way are cows and other animals of use in the religious services performed to the mighty Linga?

A.—The cow is of use on account of the five products which she yields, and the bezoar found in her stomach.

The five products of the cow are, milk, butter-milk, clarified butter, cow-dung, and water. All these things are necessary for the anointings and ablutions of the linga. Milk, clarified butter, and butter-milk are used also as offerings.

145.

Q.—In what other ways is the cow useful?

A.—The cow, and also the ox, are useful in providing hides for the heads of drums, tambourines, and other similar musical instruments used in the temple worship; and also in furnishing strings for lutes and other stringed instruments.

146.

Q.—What other animals are similarly useful?

A.—The civet-cat, and the musk-deer. The peacock is also useful for its feathers, which are made into fans.

147.

Q.—In what way is the vegetable kingdom of religious use?

A.—The plantain, jack, mango, cocoa-nut, and other similar trees, are useful for their fruits, which are required for unctions and offerings. So also the lime-tree, the orange-tree, and other trees of that class.

Some trees, shrubs, and creepers, are used in the ablutions of the god, and in the sacrifices by fire made to him.

Others are used in the flower and leaf-offerings of the temples. The flowers so used are of four classes, viz., flowers of trees; flowers of creeping-plants, such as the jasmine; water-flowers, such as the lotus and the blue and red water-lilies; and the flowers of shrubs.

A black-bird, a heron, and a swine, have obtained future happiness by offerings of sacred leaves: so also have an elephant, a serpent, a spider, a monkey, a frog, a squirrel, an ant, and some other creatures.

When saint Gnanasambanda sang an inspired hymn to change a male palmyra-tree into a female palmyra-tree at Tiruv-Ottur, that palmyra-tree also obtained future happiness.

Also when Umapati-Shivacharya, who was one of the Chandanacharyas, conferred initiation upon a thorn-bush at Chidambaram, that bush at once withered up and received future happiness.

148.

Q.—But trees and shrubs do not appear to have souls: how then are they capable of obtaining Shaiva merits and of partaking of future happiness?

A.—The eight million four hundred thousand different kinds of souls are divided into two classes, 1. Chara; 2. Achara. The Chara class consists of such as walk, fly, or creep: the Achara class consists of such as do not possess the power of locomotion. The Chara class includes the gods, men, beasts, birds, and reptiles: the Achara class contains all mountains and trees. Now these last are possessed of one of the five senses, namely, the sense of touch: and on this account they are called 'Unisensual souls.'

149.

Q.—How are the special temples which have the power of conferring Shaiva merits to be discovered?

A.—By the different local puranas, which form portions of the ten Shaiva puranas; and also by the Shaiva hymn-books, the Devaram and the Patikam.

[The Catechism concludes with a long list of the names of the Shaiva temples of note throughout India, extending over sixty pages; followed by a shorter list of Shaiva saints, whose history is connected with some of those temples.]

CPSIA information can be obtained at www.ICGtesting.com
Printed in the USA
LVOW03s1323170815

450434LV00024B/651/P